RTÉ
OFF CAMERA

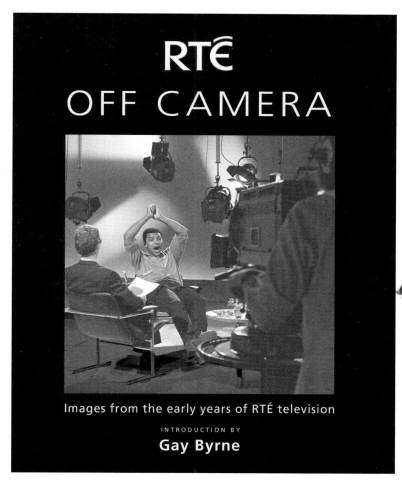

Images from the early years of RTÉ television

INTRODUCTION BY
Gay Byrne

POOLBEG

Published 2004

Poolbeg Press Ltd.
123 Grange Hill, Baldoyle,
Dublin 13,
Ireland

Email: poolbeg@poolbeg.com

1 3 5 7 9 10 8 6 4 2

A catalogue record for this book is available from the British Library.

ISBN 1 84223 213 4

Designed by Steven Hope
Typeset by Patricia Hope in Bembo 11/14

Printed by Nøhaven Book
Viborg, Denmark

www.poolbeg.com

A C K N O W L E D G E M E N T S

The RTÉ Stills Library sincerely thanks the following for their assistance in the production of this book; Bríd Dooley, Peter Feeney, Eithne Hand, Tom Holton, Emma Keogh, Brian Lynch, Adrian Moynes, Sinéad O'Connor, Pearl Quinn and Conor Sweeney.

Thanks also to Grant's Advanced Photo Lab of Baggot Street, Lensmen & Associates and to Paula Campbell and Claire McVeigh at Poolbeg.

From *snap to zap*

Some black and white thoughts for a picture phone generation

Gay Byrne

The saying goes that if you remember the sixties you probably weren't there. But I do and I was. Most of these pictures are from that decade. Though at first glance, not only do they seem like something from a different era – they seem like something from a different planet.

Today if we're really up with the play, we send and receive colour pictures using a mobile phone. To connect, we press a button and watch friends surfboarding at Bondi Beach or driving the four-wheeler or the Harley down Route 66. I'll come back to the subject of phones later.

These are stills. They won't talk to you like the ones on the picture phone and they are definitely not going to move. You can't click a mouse on them and make them come alive, but here they are, ninety or so images of what was my own living and working world four decades ago. For me it took a while to connect with some of them and I was there.

When we got television, admittedly only one-channel television, I recall the importance and significance that everybody seemed to attach to *everything* that appeared on the screen. It cannot be overstated. My memory is of people rushing home from work in the evening to look at *Bat Masterson, The High Chaparral, Have Gun Will Travel,* or, God help us, *The Fugitive*. It was great, it was new, it was exciting and it was ours. Even in the churches, the time of evening sodalities was occasionally moved (does anyone remember evening sodalities?) to suit the showing of *The Forsyte Saga*. The nation worried about the fate of the one-armed man in *The Fugitive*, or the national importance of how Jacob's got the figs into the fig rolls. Yes, really.

But it was the home-made programmes that caused the real stir, and the people who presented them that did the stirring. New ideas and new terms flowed into every living room in the country. In rapid succession we learned about poverty and illiteracy and subjects that had been taboo and were not mentioned in polite society like divorce and contraception. The first time we mentioned the remotest possibility of divorce in Ireland on *The Late Late Show* some of the audience walked out in protest. And we were merely talking about it!

Television seeped into the slow, orderly Irish world of received authority, dutiful newspaper reporting, and practically no social comment outside the four walls of a public house near closing time. In with the sixties came Bunny Carr, Terry Wogan, Charles Mitchel, Brian Farrell, Brian Cleeve and Frank Hall to educate, inform and

especially to entertain us. They quickly became household names. Not everybody was delighted with this innovation. Television bypassed the newspapers and they did not like it. Television, we were told, would do away with newspapers, make them all redundant; and they were wrong about that too.

From the day it began Telefís Éireann was very important to all of us – important to those who sat and watched, and important to those of us lucky enough to be able to make the programmes. I recall a line I used to close a *Late Late Show* in 1965, when I had a number of distinguished television critics as guests on the panel. The idea for the show was that they would lead a discussion about where Telefís Éireann was going – I hadn't banked on the studio audience and the vehemence of their opinions. At the end of the show I told that audience "We have three million critics, and they all know exactly what they want", unfortunately three million different things.

And speaking of millions, there are an estimated two million images in RTÉ's marvellous photographic archive – one for everybody in the audience perhaps? But in the way of this world, we can only fit a few score of them between the covers of one book. Professionals took all of the photos here – and most of the subjects are well used to being photographed. But there is a difference – hardly any of the pictures are posed.

Most were taken while the subjects were thinking about other things, waiting for the cameras to roll or just after a take ended. So the subjects are on duty but off-camera.

I could bang on forever about the individual images but I'll just pick out a few that prompt my memory. You can take your own time and enjoy the rest of them at your leisure! A surprising thing is that you might recognise people and places and events – but you still won't quite believe what you are seeing. For instance, look at the picture of President Kennedy speaking in Wexford in 1963. Look at the roof of the building behind him – how about that for security? Is that really Ruth Buchanan and come to think of it, what am I doing sitting in a film director's chair? And as for that 'Twist' picture – what on earth could our distinguished historian and scholar John Bowman be talking about to Chubby Checker?

Some pictures show worldwide legends like Muhammad Ali, or The Beatles who came to see us and went away again. All were talented and talent endures. Look at Twink, Vincent Browne, Rosaleen Linehan, and Mary Kenny. Some were "big in the fifties" but got lost in the sixties. Some belonged to the theatre and the variety world but did not quite adjust to the newer medium of television. But they all belonged to this world, this past planet. Most of the people are strong both in their skills and personalities – there are poets, entertainers, sculptors, actors, sporting greats and writers. Frank O'Connor, among his other claims to fame, was the first Irish writer to do a solo programme for Telefís Éireann produced by the excellent Hilton Edwards. Another O'Connor I see, Ulick of that name, excelled at boxing, pole-vaulting, law, poetry and biography – and of course as a

TV personality. Despite our occasionally stormy times on *The Late Late Show*, his contributions and those of the late Denis Franks set the tone for free-flowing, sometimes torrential discussions which left a real mark on the show for a long time.

I see my long-time friend Larry Gogan. He and I appeared in a play *The Amazing Mr Pennypacker* in the Olympia Theatre in Dublin. That was a bit before television – over the years we keep on telling lies about each other's age and the money we are making. There is a striking image of Mary Kenny, an outstanding *bête noir* of "Holy Catholic Ireland" mainly because of her feminist views. She was one of the founders of the Irish feminist movement. As a guest on my programme she was cheeky, outspoken and outrageous. Mary had been one of the crowd that went to Belfast on the famous "contraceptive train", which was met by customs men in Connolly Station. Looking back at it now it was all hilarious but at the time it was very serious. The controversy – dear God! She's writing nowadays, and so well, for *The Irish Independent* and *The Irish Catholic*.

At the time Telefís Éireann opened I was still working for Granada TV. But my great hero and friend Eamonn Andrews was appointed Chairman of the new RTÉ Authority. On opening night inside the Gresham Hotel, Eamonn presided at the ceremonies for the great and the good. We see him here setting a good example to us all by buying the first TV Licence in the GPO. Very dignified indeed. By the way, a little less dignified on that same opening night was my good friend Mr Mike Murphy, who (allegedly) was outside in freezing cold O'Connell Street pelting Michael O'Hehir with snowballs, as the unfortunate man was introducing the singer Patrick O'Hagan and the Army No 1 Band.

My brother Ernest became RTÉ's first Executive Producer. Like many others, he had come home from America to join the exciting and adventurous world of the new national television service. The story goes that something went wrong with the transmission desk on opening night. Poor Ernest had to keep his finger pressed on a button all night to keep the station on the air! The viewers never knew.

Tom McGrath was another who came home, this time from Canada. He was the man who started *The Late Late Show* – he has a lot to answer for. His daughter, Anita, is now a producer in RTÉ radio. Later on I became a newsreader on RTÉ television, and also presented the quiz programme *Jackpot*. I, of course, presented this show brilliantly, with the help of Olive White and Bart Bastable. Then I left for BBC London, and it was only when that other fella Wogan took over from me that they made a complete banjax of it!

Charles Mitchel was our first newsreader. Such was his on-screen presence, that a reader's letter to the *RTV Guide* claimed that if Charles had told us all that Martians had landed in Balbriggan we would have believed him without demur. Kathleen Watkins worked in "presentation" – she was one of the first three Telefís Éireann presenters, but wisely and prudently she used to bring her harp in to work. If there was a breakdown or a gap in the programme, she sang them a song – from the presentation studio – to keep things going. When everything was fixed up she would put the harp away and go back to making the announcements. All perfectly natural and without fuss. What about that picture of me presenting *The World of Film*? I remember Jim FitzGerald produced the programme but we could not afford decent film excerpts for it – we ended up with nothing except "arty" bits and pieces from Czechoslovakia and Poland. The film companies were not very helpful at the time.

I said I'd come back to phones − that picture of me with Charlie Roberts on *The Late Late Show* reminds me of the moon landing of 1969. Both television and radio stayed on air all through the night. I presented a live radio programme from the GPO and for the very first time on Irish radio we took telephone calls "live" on the air from people requesting music, while they were waiting for the magic moment of the moon landing. At the time, the engineers in the GPO were very much opposed to using live telephone calls on air and we had to fight to make this major

breakthrough. The next step was to use the phone live on *The Late Late Show* so we could take calls from our viewers. In its way it was another kind of milestone.

I'll leave you now to enjoy the pictures. When TV started it was so novel and magical and we were all filled with the wonder of it. The novelty is in the face of that serious young man from *School Around the Corner* trying to make sense of the EMI Image Orthicon camera in 1963. Was he looking to his future? We are looking at his past. And as far as magic is concerned, look at that happy group of children gathered around Eugene Lambert (O'Brien) and Nora O'Mahony (Godmother) and Bill Golding (Rory). Eugene himself is still packing them in, in his wonderful, magical puppet theatre in Monkstown. And, forty years on, Judge and Crow are still making the picture phone generation of children laugh. As I said before, talent endures.

What strikes me is that some of the people in these pictures are now moving to the margins of our memory. Of course, to a certain age group the pictures will bring back memories. But do any of the picture phone users remember Noel Purcell, Cecil Sheridan, Danny Cummins, Monica Sheridan and Blaithín? The sad truth is that there are now probably two generations who haven't heard of them. We're up against time in these photographs. And it's no harm to be reminded of those people who nurtured the infant television service over forty years ago.

I'm glad we have these pictures − even if we didn't get them on a mobile phone. Enjoy them.

Gay Byrne • 1963

The RTÉ Stills Library

The photographs selected for this book are but a snapshot of the larger RTÉ Stills Library holdings.

The Stills Library was established in 1967 with the aim of collecting and providing access to the photographic material produced and obtained by the station. Since then, it has developed to become a rich source of images depicting a unique record of Irish social, political and cultural life. Original images are held in different formats. These include, glass plates, negatives, lantern slides, slides, colour and black and white prints and digital. Every attempt is made to keep the Stills Library holdings up-to-date, and contemporary material is added when possible.

In 2001 the RTÉ Guide Collection of negatives was placed under the care of the Stills Library. This Collection contains outstanding photographs extending from the early years of RTÉ television to the early eighties. Most of these photographs were taken by the Guide's staff photographer, Roy Bedell. The Collection features images from early television and radio programmes, including guests, presenters and the staff involved in the production of light entertainment, drama, music and current affairs output.

In 2002 the Stills Library obtained the RTÉ Stills Department Collection. This fine Collection of negatives covers the early years of RTÉ television up to the end of 2001. The Collection, shot by the photographers staffing the RTÉ Stills Department, features stills from RTÉ television and radio programmes and of Irish personalities and events.

Alongside this material, the Stills Library has also throughout the years, acquired special Collections of photographic material. These Collections provide added value and interest to the Stills Library holdings.

The Cashman Collection, photographed by Joseph Cashman, dates from the period 1913 - 1966. The photographs provide excellent coverage of political figures and events from a turbulent epoch in Irish history. Many of these photographs illustrate the 1916 Rising, the War of Independence and the Civil War.

The Johnson Collection was shot by the English artist and photographer Nevill Johnson. In the early 1950s the Arts Council awarded him a grant towards taking a photographic record of Dublin City. From 1952-1953, he photographed what became the Johnson Collection mainly using a Leica camera.

The Murtagh Collection covers topics such as the 1916 Easter Rising, the burning of Cork city, the visit of George V to Ireland in 1911 and the 1932 Eucharistic Congress.

The Shard Collection depicts a middle class family in the South County Dublin/ County Wicklow area at the turn of the 20th century.

To permit the archiving of the original items in the Stills Library holdings, and to provide for easier browsing and retrieval, a digitisation project was initiated in 1996. To date, over 100,000 images have been digitised. As a vast number of images remain to be digitised, the digitisation of the Stills Library Collections is an ongoing process.

The Stills Library functions include a service to programmes and related back-up areas. Particular emphasis is given to the provision of material to news-related areas and to Irish and RTÉ originated material for general station use. The Stills Library also provides a full commercial service for the research and sale of photographic material to Independent Productions and other commercial bodies as well as private customers and public institutions. The Stills Library research, viewing and copying facilities are, of course, subject to the preservation and conservation status of its Collections.

Telefís Éireann's Opening Night

A series of pictures taken at the launch of Telefís Éireann on New Year's Eve 1961. The station was formally inaugurated by President Eamon de Valera. Celebrations took place in the ballroom of the Gresham Hotel from where an outside broadcast unit relayed pictures. It was snowing in Dublin that night but a large crowd still gathered outside the Gresham to welcome the new television station with the New Year.

An Taoiseach Sean Lemass as he appeared on screen during the first transmission.

Patrick O'Hagan accompanied by the No 1 Army band leads the crowd outside the Gresham Hotel in singing. Note the Pye television set on the scaffolding in the background.

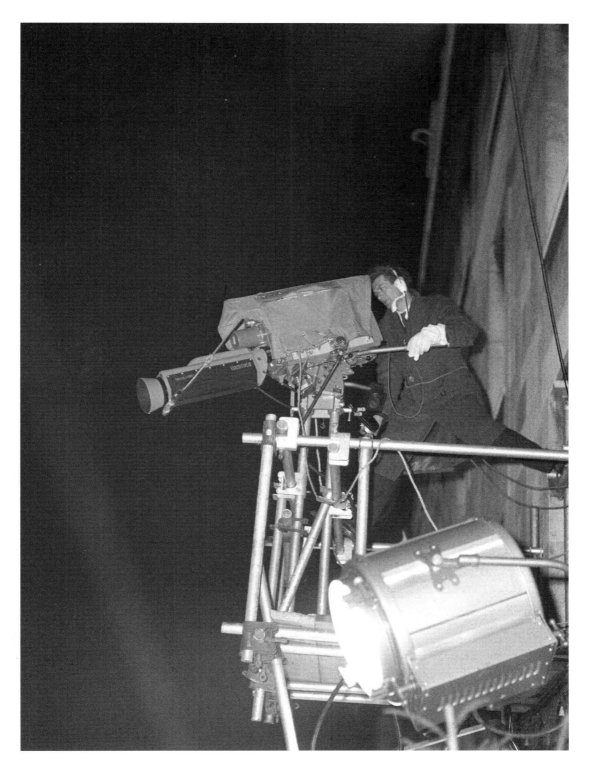

A fearless cameraman on a window ledge outside the Gresham Hotel.

Michael O'Hehir addresses the camera in the ballroom of the Gresham.

Kathleen Watkins, the first continuity announcer to appear on RTÉ television screens.

Eamonn Andrews buys his TV licence at the GPO on 2 January 1962.

The Riordans

This was one of RTÉ's most successful serials and broke new ground in using an outside broadcast unit to videotape on location rather than film in studio. Its storylines initially concentrated on agricultural matters but it soon branched out into more social issues.

James Douglas wrote the first twenty-four episodes; Wesley Burrowes took over subsequently. *The Riordans* ran until 1979.

Moira Deady as Mary Riordan, Tom Hickey as Benjy Riordan and Rebecca Wilkinson as Jude Riordan in a scene from the very first episode broadcast on 4 January 1965.

John Cowley as Tom Riordan • 1965

Tom Hickey as Benjy Riordan • 1965

Joe Pilkington as Eamon Maher • 1971

The wedding of Benjy Riordan and Maggie Nael, who was played by Biddy White-Lennon. Rebecca Wilkinson as Jude Riordan can be seen in the right background • 1973

Tolka Row

This drama serial was set in a new corporation housing estate on the north side of Dublin, and ran from 1964 to 1968. The story centred on the lives of the Nolan family, their neighbours and workmates. Comparable to *Coronation Street* across the water, *Tolka Row* ended in 1968 with the emigration of its two central characters, Jack and Rita Nolan.

Jim Bartley as Sean Nolan and Brenda Fricker as Joan Broderick, during filming in 1967. Jim Bartley currently plays Bela Doyle in RTÉ's *Fair City*; Jim celebrated 40 years with RTÉ in 2004. Brenda Fricker won a Best Supporting Actress Oscar in 1990 for her role in *My Left Foot*.

May Ollis as Rita Nolan (first left), Des Perry as Jack Nolan and Aileen Harte as Assumpta Feeney, also in a 1967 edition of *Tolka Row*.

From left to right; May Ollis, the late Iris Lawler as Statia Nolan and Laurie Morton as Peggy Nolan, also in 1967.

Anita Reeves as Nuala Brosnan and Donal Cox as Colm Maher, on the set of the RTÉ television series *Southside* in 1969. This was a suburban drama serial set in Cork, written by David Hayes and produced by Deirdre Friel. It ran for one year under the title *Southside*, and for a second season as *Newpark Southside* before ending in 1970.

Cyril Cusack as Anglo-Irish landowner Sir Jonah Barrington in *I Stood Well With All Parties*, a programme in the *Facets Irish* series, broadcast on 18 April 1972. *Facets Irish* examined the literary heritage associated with different parts of Ireland. Louis Lentin produced this programme which featured Cyril Cusack reading from Barrington's memoirs.

John Cowley (left, as Dr Canty) and Aiden Grennell as Dr Knock on the set of the television play *An Apple a Day* in July 1963. This play was translated by Mícheál Mac Liammóir from the original French comic play *Knock* by Jules Romains. It was produced by Christopher Fitz-Simon. Note the precarious window frame and boom microphone overhead!

Donal McCann in *Land*, an adaptation by Adrian Vale of the Liam O'Flaherty novel. Set during the Irish land wars of the late nineteenth century, this eight-part series was broadcast in 1967. The producer/director was Louis Lentin.

Mícheál Mac Liammóir at his Harcourt Terrace home in early 1964. This photograph was taken as part of a publicity shoot for *The Importance of Being Oscar*, Mac Liammoir's one-man show based on the life and works of Oscar Wilde. It was first televised by RTÉ on St Patrick's Day 1964 with Chloe Gibson producing and Hilton Edwards, RTÉ's then Head of Drama, presenting.

Irish actress Siobhán McKenna with her son Donnchadha O'Dea, in their Dublin home in 1966. A still from this shoot was used in a brief article in the *RTÉ Guide* of 11 November 1966, to publicise McKenna's presentation of the programme *Iar Phroinn*. This was essentially an after-dinner studio discussion in Irish, with a different host and guests each week. Donnchadha O'Dea was one of his mother's guests on the programme broadcast on 12 November 1966, which was produced by Charles Scott.

Insurrection

This series, made to mark the 50th anniversary of the Easter Rising, was a major undertaking by RTÉ. Written by Hugh Leonard, it was broadcast in eight half-hour parts on consecutive nights, over Easter Week 1966. It adopted an innovative format; the dramatisations of actual events were framed by eyewitness-style news reports. The series was shot on both film and television cameras on location and in studio. There were over eighty speaking parts in *Insurrection* and many more extras, including members of the Irish Army. The producer/director was Louis Lentin.

Eoin Ó Súilleabháin as Patrick Pearse under arrest at Kilmainham Gaol.

Extras playing members of Cumann na mBan tend injured volunteers. The interior of the GPO was reconstructed (and burned) in RTÉ's Studio 1.

Eoin Ó Súilleabháin observes the burning GPO set.

A fireman extinguishes the flames.

Children wait in their classroom for *Telefís Scoile* to begin in October 1968. *Telefís Scoile* comprised several different series of programmes on subjects studied by secondary school students at Intermediate and Leaving Certificate levels. It was initiated by RTÉ in 1964 in association with the Department of Education.

Three members of the *Wanderly Wagon* cast surrounded by young fans in the grounds of RTÉ in 1969. Bill Golding as Rory, Nora O'Mahony as Godmother and Eugene Lambert as O'Brien are all visible in this shot which was taken for the *RTÉ Guide*. *Wanderly Wagon* ran on RTÉ from 1967 to 1982 – the original wagon can now be seen at the National Museum, Collins Barracks, Dublin.

Nora O'Mahony as Godmother and Eugene Lambert as O'Brien, in a publicity still for the RTÉ children's television series *Wanderly Wagon*, in November 1971. Two of the puppets which featured in the show are also visible in this shot; Mr Crow is looking over Godmother's shoulder and Eugene Lambert is holding Judge the Dog.

Let's Draw with Blaithín Ní Chnaimhín in 1967. Blaithín also presented an earlier arts and crafts programme for children in 1963, entitled *Ceapars*.

A young camera operator on *School Around the Corner* in 1962. This programme was presented by schoolteacher Paddy Crosbie and first ran on RTÉ television from 1962 to 1967. The writer James Plunkett produced the programme during this period.

The *School Around the Corner* 1963 Easter Party, held in RTÉ's Donnybrook studios for the 172 children who were interviewed on the programme during the year. Highlights from this party were shown on the programme televised on Easter Sunday.

11-year old Tony Finnegan of Hardwicke Street, Dublin, performing at the 1963 Easter Party. Note accordionist Thelma Ramsey in the right background – she provided accompaniment for the children's party pieces.

Paddy Crosbie talks to children during the recording of an episode broadcast in late 1962.

Nelson's Pillar from the roof of the GPO in O'Connell Street shortly after the bomb explosion which destroyed it on 8th March 1966. RTÉ had radio studios in the GPO until 1973 and the roof of the building was a popular location for RTÉ publicity shots. The Pillar was one of Dublin's most famous landmarks. Irish army engineers blew up the remainder of the monument two days after the initial explosion.

Former Irish film censor and former RTÉ cameraman Sheamus Smith, setting up a shot with a 16mm film camera outside the Irish Life Centre in Dublin's Mespil Road in 1963. He was filming an interview broadcaster Arthur Murphy was conducting with American singer Pat Boone for *Kino*, a programme about film.

US President John F Kennedy is conferred with the freedom of Wexford town by the Lord Mayor Councillor Thomas Byrne during his visit to Ireland in June 1963. Also visible on the official stand are Brendan Corish leader of the Labour Party (immediately to the left of the President), Lee Radziwill, (Jackie Kennedy's sister), Jean Kennedy Smith, and Frank Aiken, Minister for Foreign Affairs who is seated to the right, applauding. Just five months after this picture was taken Kennedy was assassinated in Dallas, Texas.

RTÉ's first newsreader Charles Mitchel in the newsroom in 1972. He read the first news bulletin for the station on Telefís Éireann's opening night on New Year's Eve 1961.

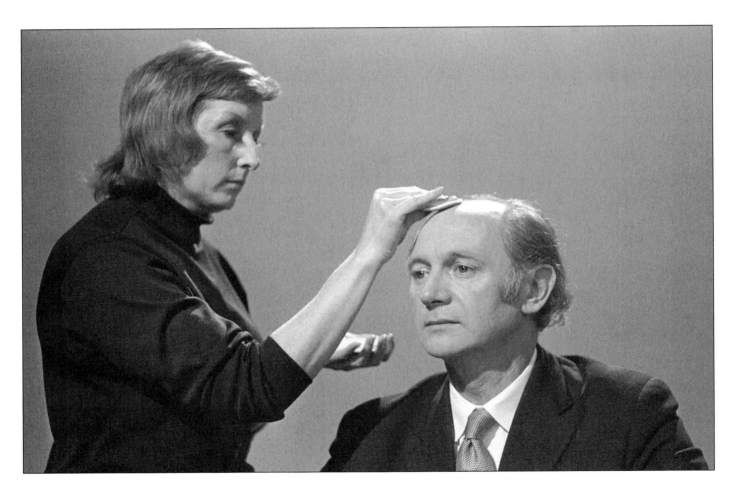

RTÉ make-up artist Maureen Carter prepares Fianna Fáil Taoiseach Jack Lynch for a party political broadcast in November 1972. This programme would have aired in early 1973 ahead of that year's general election held on 28 February.

Broadcaster Brian Farrell (left) interviews Irish writer and politician Conor Cruise O'Brien, on the set of the RTÉ television current affairs programme *7 Days* in 1973. O'Brien had just been appointed Minister for Posts and Telegraphs in the Fine Gael/Labour coalition government of 1973-77. Farrell interviewed him about the future of RTÉ for *7 Days*.

Bishop Fulton Sheen (1895-1979) auxiliary bishop of New York, strikes a pose in an RTÉ television studio in 1968. Bishop Sheen, who was known as America's 'television bishop', recorded a forty minute talk aimed at young people for broadcast by RTÉ. Producer Denis O'Grady observed in an *RTÉ Guide* article how comfortable Bishop Sheen was with the medium, ". . . here was a man who knew more about television than I could hope to learn in the next ten years." The man behind the camera is future Eurovision-winning songwriter Shay Healy.

Fr James McDyer, parish priest of Glencolumbkille, Co. Donegal with a young parishioner in 1971. Fr McDyer initiated a number of co-operative projects in farming and textiles aimed at regenerating this part of Donegal. He talked about his work in the RTÉ television documentary series *Report*.

Three inhabitants of Gola Island, off the coast of County Donegal, in October 1969. This still was taken during the filming of the RTÉ documentary *Terminus*, about the decline and depopulation of the island.

Terminus was first broadcast by RTÉ television on 30 January 1970 with Odran Walsh producing. RTÉ also commissioned a book in conjunction with this film entitled *Gola: The life and last days of an island community*, by FHA Aalen and H Brody. Fr James McDyer reviewed the book for the *RTÉ Guide* of 23 January 1970.

A man mends nets by his fireside in Gola Island, October 1969.

Broadcaster and journalist Patrick Gallagher interviews Mrs Catherine Sexton of Dublin, on the way to Knock Shrine in County Mayo, on 23 August 1970. The interview took place on board the Dublin to Claremorris train. This still was one of a series taken for a programme about the shrine entitled, *There's Something About Knock*. It was broadcast as part of the *Report* documentary series on 29 October 1970, with John Williams producing. The *RTÉ Guide* published an article by *Morning Ireland* presenter David Hanly on the programme in October 1970.

Broadcaster John O'Donoghue talks to children in Cherry Orchard for a *7 Days* programme on travellers in 1968.

A striking image of a young girl on that same encampment. Her "house" can be seen in the left background.

American popular singer and originator of "The Twist" dance craze Chubby Checker (centre, real name Ernest Evans) is interviewed by RTÉ broadcaster John Bowman (left) at a reception in the Gresham Hotel, Dublin in July 1963. The *RTV Guide* published a feature on Checker's visit to Dublin in its edition of 26 July.

The wedding of Gay Byrne and Kathleen Watkins in Saggart, Co. Dublin in 1963.

Twink (Adele King) at 12. This was a shot taken to publicise her appearance on the children's television programme *Seoirse agus Beartlaí* in the early 1960s.

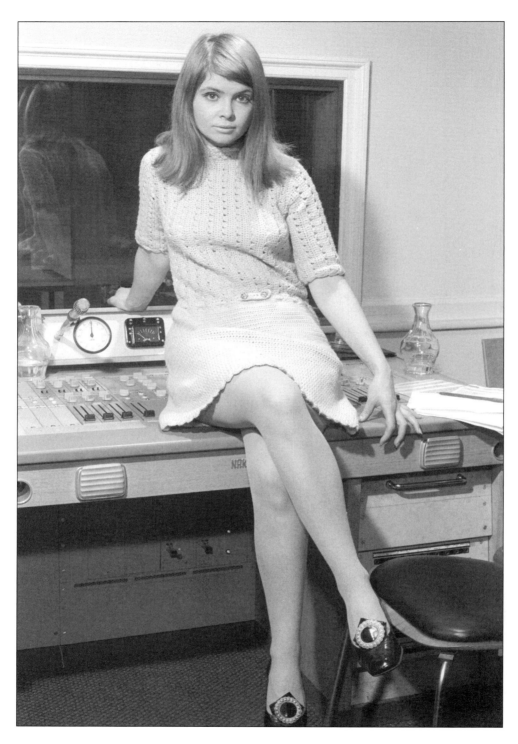

Broadcaster Ruth Buchanan models a crochet mini-dress for the *RTÉ Guide* in 1968, shortly after she joined the station as a continuity announcer.

Journalist and broadcaster Vincent Browne in 1967. This picture was taken on the set of *Roundabout Now*, a summer magazine programme – Browne was one of the programme's reporters.

Journalist Mary Kenny in 1969. She was a reporter on the late night radio programme *Later than Late* at the time this picture was taken.

Máire Ní Bhraonáin of Clannad performing in the 1975 *Pan-Celtic Song Contest*. Clannad were selected to represent Ireland in the international competition held in Killarney, County Kerry. The Killarney contest featured entries from the six Celtic regions of Ireland, Scotland, Brittany, the Isle of Man, Cornwall and Wales.

Irish folk group The Johnstons performing in RTÉ's Studio 2 during the recording of the television series *Imeall* in late 1969. From left to right Mick Moloney, Adrienne Johnston and singer/songwriter Paul Brady. *Imeall* was an Irish language pop music show presented by Sean Bán Breathnach and produced by Jeremy Swan. The first programme, which featured The Johnstons, was broadcast on 8 January 1970.

Broadcaster Larry Gogan, dressed as a pirate for an *RTV Guide* competition, in 1964. This shot was taken for a Christmas "Who's Who" competition in the Guide. Six television personalities in all were disguised.

Gay Byrne in a publicity shot for *The World of Film* in 1964, an RTÉ programme he presented while commuting between Dublin and Granada TV in Manchester.

Terry Wogan with co-presenter (and fashion model) Suzanne MacDougald on the set of an early television quiz show *Jackpot* in 1965. Gay Byrne first presented the show with model Olive White.

Gay Byrne with floor manager Charlie Roberts on the set of *The Late Late Show* in the late 1960s, checking the phone before going on air. *The Late Late* was the first television programme to use telephone calls live on air.

Gay Byrne with Granny Connors on *The Late Late Show* traveller special in 1969.

Fran O'Toole of The Miami Showband with Dana Rosemary Scallon in 1972. This was a publicity shot for the programme *Dana*, a music series set in the 1930s. Fran O'Toole was tragically shot dead by the UVF along with two other members of 'The Miami' (Brian McCoy and Anthony Geraghty) while returning to the Republic from a gig in Banbridge, Co Down in July 1975.

Jimmy O'Dea with the late Maureen Potter in a sketch from *The Life and Times of Jimmy O'Dea* broadcast on Christmas Day 1964. The sketches were written by Harry O'Donovan. The producer James Plunkett won a Jacob's award for this programme.

Cameramen enjoying the produce of *Monica Sheridan's Kitchen* in 1963. From left to right, Paul Gleeson, Aidan Maguire and Eugene Barrington.

American film actor Lee Marvin on Dublin's O'Connell Street in 1966. He may have been in town to promote the film *Cat Ballou*; Frank Hall interviewed him for the countrywide current affairs programme *Newsbeat*.

RTÉ's former Head of Drama (1961-64) Hilton Edwards (left) presents Frank Hall with a Jacob's Award, "for his expertise in dealing with matters of town and country" on *Newsbeat* in 1966.

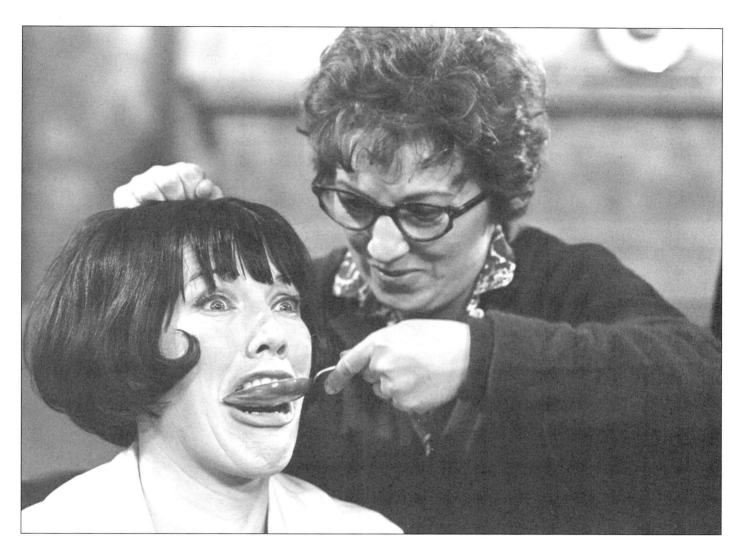

Rosaleen Linehan (left) and Maureen Potter, in a scene from *Me and My Friend*, RTÉ television's first home-grown situation comedy series, during filming in 1967. Fergus Linehan was the writer and Jim FitzGerald the producer.

Michael O'Hehir playing football with his 4-year old daughter Ann in the garden of their Dublin home in September 1964. A still from this shoot was used on the front of the *RTV Guide* to publicise RTÉ's coverage of that year's All-Ireland football final between Galway and Kerry.

RTÉ sports announcer Brendan O'Reilly, clears a tennis net at the Iveagh Sports Grounds, Crumlin in Dublin in May 1963. O'Reilly was an accomplished athlete – he was the Irish high jump champion at the time this picture was taken. A picture from this shoot was used on the front cover of the *RTV Guide*.

RTÉ cameraman Phil Mulally, on the pitch at Croke Park just before the start of the All-Ireland Senior Hurling Final between Cork and Kilkenny, on 7 September 1969. He is walking towards the goal mouth, carrying a mobile camera and with a power pack strapped to his back.

British jockey Lester Piggott kisses the horse Ribocco, shortly after winning the Irish Sweeps Derby at the Curragh, County Kildare on 1 July 1967. Michael Smith, probably the horse's trainer/owner, is standing on the left of shot. The Irish Sweeps Derby was worth over £80,000 at the time, making it one of the world's richest races. Jacqueline Kennedy Onassis visited the Curragh on the day of the Derby.

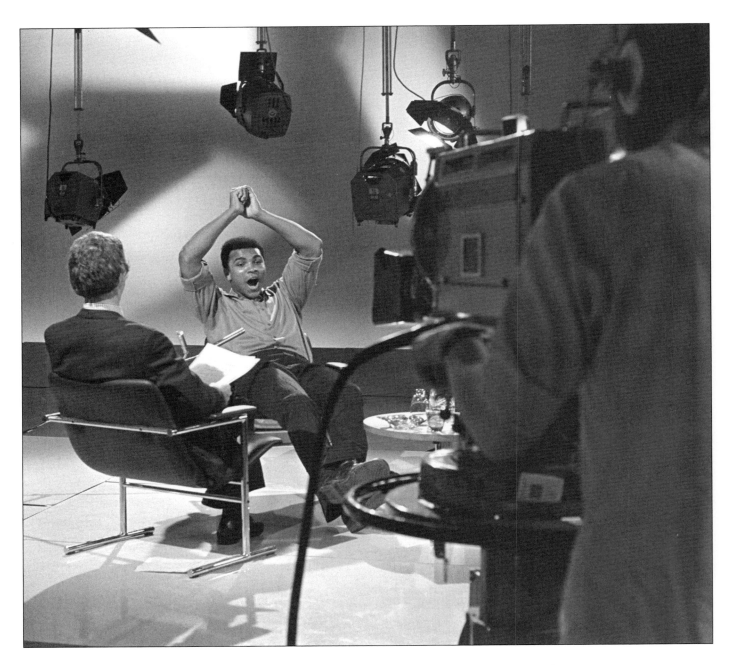

Muhammad Ali with Cathal O'Shannon in an infamous bout from 1972. This interview was broadcast the evening before Ali's fight with Al "Blue" Lewis at Croke Park on 19th July. Photographer Tom Holton found the charisma of Ali was noticeable as soon as he entered the room; in spite of his fame he was a warm and gentle man who stayed until well after the recording of the interview to talk and sign autographs for the crew (including one on the studio wall!). Ali is also seen here on *Sport in Action* with Michael O'Hehir also from 1972.

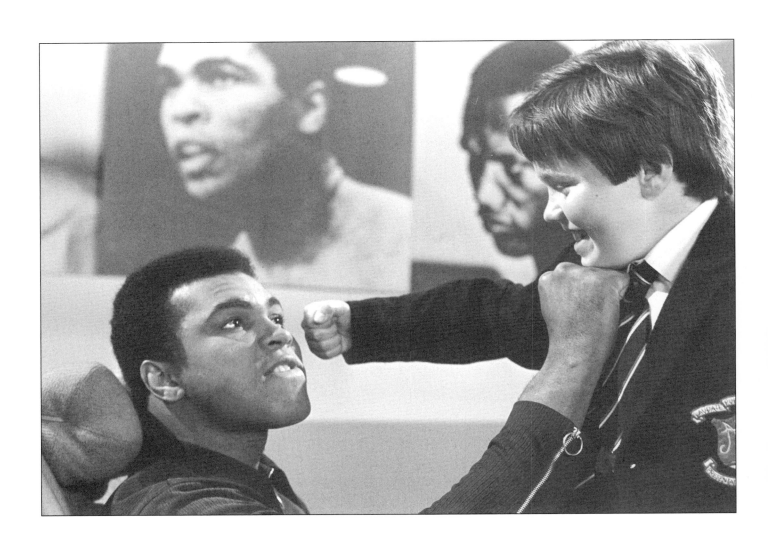

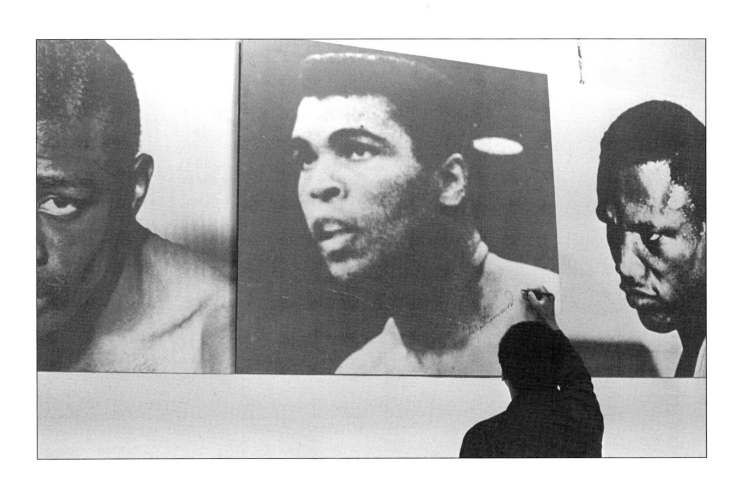

The Beatles played two evening concerts at the Adelphi Cinema on Abbey Street in November 1963, where they were greeted by hordes of screaming fans. Earlier that afternoon they were interviewed by Paul Russell, presenter of RTÉ television's *The Showband Show*. This interview was filmed by Bill Robinson in the ballroom of the Gresham Hotel where the group stayed while in Dublin.

Joe Dolan performing on *The Go 2 Show*, during recording in the summer of 1967. Dolan was guitarist and lead singer with The Drifters at the time. *The Go 2 Show* was broadcast weekly and featured some of the best-known Irish showbands. The first programme was broadcast on 25 July 1967 with Adrian Cronin producing. Among the regular presenters were Larry Gogan, BP Fallon and Mike Murphy.

Irish singer Dickie Rock, performing with The Miami Showband on *The Go 2 Show*, during recording in the summer of 1967.

Butch Moore on the same show, also in 1967. Butch had been the lead singer with the Capitol Showband – he had gone solo by the time this programme was recorded. He was also Ireland's first Eurovision Song Contest entrant, coming in sixth place with *Walking the Streets in the Rain* (1965).

Dancers Olivia Burke and John O'Sullivan, performing on RTE television's pop music show *Like Now!*, during recording in Dun Laoghaire's Top Hat Ballroom in 1968. The duo appeared weekly on the show, usually dancing to American hits. *Like Now!* was presented by DJ Danny Hughes and produced by Bill Keating. The show featured Irish groups, showbands and British pop groups. The first programme was broadcast on 28 September 1968.

The Bachelors pop group, performing on *Nightlife*, a television variety programme broadcast on St Stephen's Day 1968. The show was presented by Terry Wogan and produced by Burt Budin

The Bay City Rollers performing on *The Tony Kenny Show* in 1976. The group was a precursor to the boy bands of the 1990s. They were from Scotland and wore tartan trousers and scarves as part of their act. They enjoyed a brief period of phenomenal success in the mid–1970s when Phil Coulter co-wrote many of their hits with Bill Martin.

Scottish comedian Billy Connolly singing and playing acoustic guitar on *Capital Folk* in early 1972. Billy Connolly started his career as a folk musician, initially as part of the duo, The Humblebums, and subsequently as a solo act. He released a solo album in 1972 entitled *Billy Connolly Live!*

Capital Folk was an RTÉ/BBC Scotland co-production. The programmes from Ireland were recorded in Dublin's Old Shieling. The presenters were Mike Murphy in Dublin and Lesley Blair in Edinburgh.

Uilleann piper Seamus Ennis playing on *Seamus Ennis sa Chathaoir* in late 1963. This programme featured Ennis exchanging songs and music with young people in an RTÉ television studio.

Luke Kelly, singer with Irish traditional music group The Dubliners, taking part in a session in Dublin's Church Street Club in May 1963. The Church Street Club was formed in 1956 around a core of Sligo/Leitrim musicians who had moved to Dublin. Many notable musicians from all over the country participated in sessions there. Ciarán Bourke can be seen on the right of shot, playing the tin whistle.

The Dubliners in a temporary Radio Éireann studio located in O'Connell Hall, opposite the Gresham Hotel, in Dublin's O'Connell Street. The group was there to record an item for *Ballads of a Saturday*, a fifteen-minute programme broadcast on Saturday mornings on Radio Eireann, introduced by the American folk singer Dick Cameron. The Dubliners have appeared on many RTÉ programmes over the years and had their own television series in 1970.

The original Planxty line-up performing on the television programme *Capital Folk* in early 1972. From left to right, Donal Lunny, Liam Óg O'Flynn, Andy Irvine and Christy Moore. The group split in 1975 but re-formed in 1978 and recorded three further albums, before again breaking up in 1981 when Moore and Lunny left to form Moving Hearts.

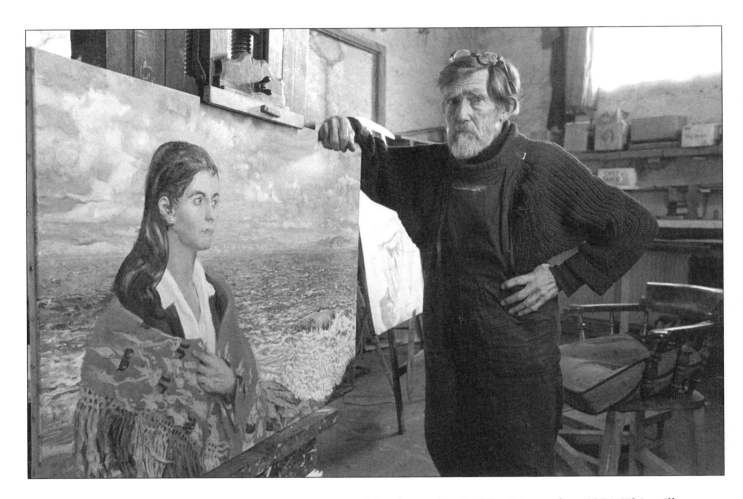

Irish artist Seán Keating in his studio in Rathfarnham, Co. Dublin, November 1971. This still was taken during the filming of an interview with Keating conducted by Colm Ó Briain, which was shown on the RTÉ television arts/documentary series *Aurora* on 23 November 1971. The painting is entitled *Young Lady Connemara Seascape*.

Seán Keating is also seen here painting the Ardnacrusha hydroelectric scheme in 1920s, in an image from the RTÉ Stills Library Cashman Collection.

Republican Dan Breen poses for John Behan in the grounds of St John of God's Hospital, Stillorgan, County Dublin in 1967. This still was taken during the filming of an interview with Breen, conducted by Jack White for RTÉ television. It was broadcast on 23 September 1967 with Aindreas Ó Gallchóir producing.

Dan Breen participated in the first engagement with British forces in the War of Independence in 1919, at Soloheadbeg in County Tipperary. He was elected a TD for Tipperary in 1923 and was the first anti-Treaty deputy to take his seat in 1927.

Sculptor Seamus Murphy, working on a portrait bust in his Cork studio on 4 July 1969. This still was taken during the filming of Seán Ó Mordha's documentary on the sculptor entitled *Stone Mad*. It was screened as part of the *Anthology* series of programmes on the arts. Murphy sculpted public monuments and figures for church buildings as well as a number of portrait busts – note the busts of Michael Collins and Sean Lemass in the background.

Novelist and short-story writer Mary Lavin at her Dublin home in 1968. She was interviewed by Niall Sheridan for the *Writer in Profile* series, which was produced by James Plunkett and broadcast on 19 November 1968.

Mary Lavin was born in Massachusetts of Irish parents and moved to Ireland as a child. She is known primarily as a short-story writer but also published two novels, *The House in Clewe Street* (1945) and *Mary O'Grady* (1950).

Frank O'Connor in Studio 2 in December 1964, during the filming of *The Forgotten Child*, his reminiscence of a childhood Christmas in Cork. The programme was broadcast on Christmas Day 1964 with James Plunkett producing. Frank O'Connor also featured in Telefís Éireann's first arts/documentary series *Self Portrait* on 2 January 1962.

Edna O'Brien is interviewed by Niall Sheridan for *Writer in Profile* in 1970. This programme was broadcast ten years after the furore that greeted the publication of her first novel *The Country Girls*. O'Brien's most recent novel at the time of this interview was *August is a Wicked Month* (1965).

Irish poet, playwright and novelist Austin Clarke, on Dublin's St Stephen's Green North, in the spring of 1967. This still was taken during the filming of RTÉ producer Adrian Cronin's film on Clarke entitled simply *Austin Clarke*. It was broadcast on 29 January 1968 as part of the series *The Writers*. UCD Professor of English Augustine Martin wrote and narrated the commentary. Austin Clarke hosted Radio Éireann's weekly poetry programme from 1942-55. He was also a guest in the Gresham Hotel on Telefís Éireann's opening night.

Irish writer and primary school teacher Bryan McMahon, on the set of the RTÉ television Irish language programme *Iar Phroinn* in 1966. Siobhán McKenna also featured in an edition of this Irish language after-dinner chat show.

Bryan McMahon taught in Listowel, County Kerry for nearly fifty years. He wrote short stories, plays and a novel, *Children of the Rainbow* (1952). His school featured in *Meet the People*, Telefís Éireann's introduction to the new television service, which featured the station's first three continuity announcers touring Ireland.

Ulick O'Connor in a still taken to illustrate his *RTV Guide* article on the Muhammad Ali v Sonny Liston fight, published on 21 February 1964. Ulick had been British universities boxing champion in 1950 and was Irish pole vault champion from 1947 to 1951. He has written biographies of Oliver St John Gogarty (1964) and Brendan Behan (1970), as well as plays and poetry. Ulick O'Connor was a regular panellist on *The Late Late Show* in the 1960s.

Patrick Kavanagh on the arts programme *Spectrum* in 1964. He read from his recently published *Collected Poems* for the programme – he is seen holding that book here. Kavanagh wrote a regular weekly column for the *RTV Guide* in the 1960s. The piece of sculpture seen in the background was part of the Living Art exhibition which also featured on this edition of *Spectrum*.

Siobhán McKenna as Nora Burke, in the JM Synge play *In the Shadow of the Glen*, broadcast by RTÉ in 1964. This production was produced and directed by Louis Lentin.

Index of Photographers

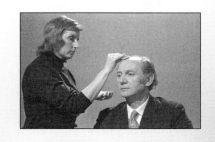

Roy Bedell

PHOTOGRAPHS

page

Joseph Cashman

PHOTOGRAPHS

page

Peter Dorney

PHOTOGRAPHS

page

54-55
80

Phil Dowling

PHOTOGRAPHS

page

51
52

Des Gaffney

RTÉ

PHOTOGRAPHS

page

Dakki Heuvelink

PHOTOGRAPHS

page

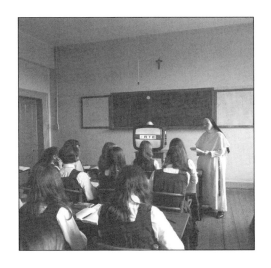

Eve Holmes

Tom Holton

Lensmen & Associates

P H O T O G R A P H S

p a g e

9
11 - 16

Eddie McEvoy

P H O T O G R A P H S

p a g e

33 - 37
48

Index

RTÉ